BURNING HOUSE

BURNING HOUSE

poems

by Richard Lemm

Wolsak and Wynn

© Richard Lemm, 2010

No part of this publication may be reproduced, stored in a retrieval system or transmitted, in any form or by any means, without the prior written consent of the publisher or a license from The Canadian Copyright Licensing Agency (Access Copyright). For an Access Copyright license, visit www.accesscopyright.ca or call toll free to 1-800-893-5777.

Cover image: *Vertigo* by Adam Sultan
Author's photograph: Lee Ellen Pottie
Cover design: Leigh Kotsilidis
Typset in Minion Pro
Printed by Coach House Books Toronto, Canada

  Canadian Patrimoine
Heritage canadien

The publisher gratefully acknowledges the support of the Canada Council for the Arts, the Ontario Arts Council and the Canada Book Fund for their financial assistance.

The author gratefully acknowledges the support of the Canada Council for the Arts.

Wolsak and Wynn Publishers Ltd.
#102–69 Hughson Street North
Hamilton, ON
Canada L8R 1G5

Library and Archives Canada Cataloguing in Publication

Lemm, Richard, 1946-
Burning house / Richard Lemm.

Poems.
ISBN 978-1-894987-40-0

I. Title.

PS8573.E547B87 2010   C811'.54   C2009-907208-4

for

LEE ELLEN

CONTENTS

I HEROES

- 13 IN THE FIFTIES
- 15 WE BUILT BEAUTIFUL
- 16 WHERE WERE YOU?
- 17 PERIL
- 18 HEROES: FROM THE BURNING HOUSE
- 20 HEROES: THE DRILL
- 22 WHO TOLD YOU
- 25 SADDLEBAGS
- 27 GRADE TEN WORLD HISTORY LESSON
- 29 I LIKED IKE (AND DICK, TOO)
- 31 MY COUNTRY
- 33 FOOTNOTE FOR THE INCIDENT IN THE POTOMAC
- 34 EULOGY FOR A DRAFT BOARD
- 36 I'LL BE GONE
- 39 THE QUAY OF REGRET
- 41 RICHARD SPEAKS TO ME, THE FAINT-HEARTED

II PATRIOTS

- 45 PATRIOTS I: LOOKING UP, LOOKING DOWN
- 47 PATRIOTS II: SOFTENING
- 50 FIVE THINGS DISGUSTED HIM
- 51 HENDRIX OF ARABIA
- 52 TO CASTRO ON HIS 80TH BIRTHDAY
- 53 IN THE BEGINNING
- 55 AGAIN, THE PSALM
- 56 WASTED BREATH
- 57 AIRSPACE
- 58 BOATMEN OF ARBEIA
- 60 CHONGCHON / SAIGON / BAGHDAD
- 62 RETRIBUTION
- 63 THE TRUE MEANING OF HONOUR
- 65 THE PYRAMIDS

III WHAT I WANTED TO BE

69 ANNUNCIATION
71 WHAT I WANTED TO BE
73 TRAIL
76 WHERE YOU COME IN
78 PILGRIMAGE
82 ALAMO
85 WHAT MY MOTHER SAYS ON THE NURSING HOME PHONE
87 THE DAY AFTER
89 FOR YOUR LOSS
91 NEWLY DEAD
96 FAITH, HOPE AND

IV BERLIN FOLLIES

99 DALÍ IN FLORIDA
102 IN THE VINCENT PRICE ROOM, JOURNEY'S END
104 MEDITATION IN THE GARDEN IN THE GULF
106 BRIDE OF THE CAPTURED EARTH
107 FREELY, SING
109 AFTER THE STARSHIPS
111 LOAD AND LOCK
112 ACTAEON
114 CURTAIN
115 THE PURRING YOU HEAR
118 BERLIN FOLLIES

123 ACKNOWLEDGEMENTS

HEROES

IN THE FIFTIES

I am going to stop the war
this time. I have filled one hundred
balloons with water, cached the ammo

in my backyard shed, should
Smitty's gang show up and dare,
once more, invade our neighbourhood.

My dog's cute tricks and playful leaps
disarm most everyone, but his teeth
are sharpened on a grizzly's bones.

Grandma's laundry on the line flaps
truce, and the cherry blossoms, peace,
until the birds, fruit ripening, force

me to the BB gun. The general
in the White House left his Jeeps,
his aide-de-camp and combat boots

for drivers, putters, spike-soled shoes.
I've given up my six-guns, spurs,
for a baseball glove, swapped my sword

for a crucifix like Ben-Hur, I'll turn
the other cheek, and cross myself, unless
I'm elbowed on the basketball court.

Bearded men are landing, armed,
in a mangrove swamp, while the rat pack
parties at nightclubs in Havana.

Ronnie Reagan, celluloid cowboy,
with his General Electric pitchman smile,
says, "Progress is

our most important product."
A coloured blues guitarist, about to fry
but innocent, is saved, along with justice,

by Perry Mason in a court of law.
Another kind but tough Canuck
spreads bonanzas of common sense

across his ranch; his sons never once say *fuck*.
Oil means James Dean, stud, smouldering
near a Texas rig, and sweet young sexy Liz.

I'm no longer killing Indians or Mexicans,
leaving Davy Crockett far behind, I'm
sailing with Ahab, floating down river

on Huck and Jim's raft, riding a motorcycle
with Brando, chauffeuring that most famous blond
to the brand new and endless, final frontier.

WE BUILT BEAUTIFUL

All morning we built beautiful
bridges over streams trickling
from pools of last night's booming cloudbursts.
Pyramids of pebbles for foundations,
alder twigs for spans, poplar leaves
for pavement which our visions of tiny
sports cars, safari Jeeps, rock and roll star
limousines, and army tanks could cruise
across. The waterways below
teemed with yachts and tugs and PT
boats invisible to all but our godlike
engineering eyes. What my grandfather wanted
to be, back when a Sunday drive
through the magical air suspended
above a river or canyon was arching
proof of our brilliant, unstoppable, near-
divinity. That was after the war
and the drop and drift from soaring
inventions, my father harnessed to
white silk blooming, descending
on strangers with gifts of grenades.

We argued later, blamed each other
for starting it up. One of us, then
another, arms locked outward in rigid
wings, climbing, circling (steady
drones from our throat), then diving,
our faces in our cockpits, gleeful.
We locked on our targets and fired
stone after stone at those bridges.
Nazis trapped in their black sedans,
tough-luck sailors in their battleships,
it's wartime after all, and Rommel's tanks
fleeing back to the desert. I flew
home triumphant for soup and sandwiches,
strangely not hungry, but restless,
the ground rushing up at
me, wondering how long I could wait
to pull the parachute cord.

WHERE WERE YOU?

Jody, a Jehovah's Witness, tightly held
a gallon jar of formaldehyde. The year before,
her older sister, ill, needed blood
transfusions, and, for religious reasons, died.
The principal was speaking on the intercom,
his words packed neat and tight.
A Russian ship, its warmonger cargo of bombs,
kept steaming toward Cuba. Our ships would shoot
a warning across its bow. Communists, fearing
no god, we were told, and wanting to conquer
the world, would without conscience incinerate
millions. We froze. The PA voice
tiptoed through the rooms and halls
like a thief, or the Ripper. The Soviets' choice:
stop, be searched, or blown to smithereens,
an act of war. Helpful lab assistant
I said *nuclear*. A girl screamed,
Jody dropped the jar, it burst, sent
forth its fumes, all hell broke loose.
The windows, opened, welcomed October
air, shouts from the football field, raucous
squabble of crows. Before the truce,
we carried those passed out from formaldehyde
fumes down flights of stairs
to the lawn, the blue sky clear
of bombers, blinding lights. Our saviour
with his Irish luck and his god on a cross.
Next day, with the football team, I donated
blood, proud American. Adrenalin pumping
under my pads Friday night on the sideline.
We faced the flag while a passionate voice
launched upward and bloomed with the anthem.
My mind briefly not on the game
but on Jody's limp body in my arms
on the stairway, in the all-clear air.
Then the opening kickoff, breaking the huddle,
and I glared at my rival, sneering back,
hair-triggered on the scrimmage line.

PERIL

"It's not the end of the world,"
said my grandmother, crimping
the edges of the pie together
and gashing the crust for steam to escape.

"We thought the end was upon us
when the Germans, then British, used gas.
Then long-range artillery, and airplanes.
My own husband flying, dropping bombs,

leaned out his cockpit to see the Earth explode."
She opens the oven, tilts back
from the heat, slides Mount Apple
along the rack. "Then we were rippled

with fear, kamikazes at Pearl Harbour,
rockets landing in London and who knew
where next, Seattle?" She gets a tonic water
bottle and shakes it, says, "*Blitzkrieg*," unscrews

the top, fizz everywhere. "It settles,"
she says, pouring, and adding gin.
"Now you have those mushroom clouds,
the ships, the planes, on collision course

on the high seas, in mid-air,
but, my age? You'll say *remember when*."
The kitchen air, swelling, heats
up like the last days of Eden.

HEROES: FROM THE BURNING HOUSE

The samurai looks insignificant
beside his armor of black dragon scales.
  – Tomas Tranströmer

My warrior heroes wore spurs
and cowboy hat, perhaps a cape,
usually a gun or sword,
a godspeed talisman – a plain
bandana from a rancher's widow
or a noblewoman's indigo silk scarf –
sometimes a mask that let the eyes
insinuate vengeance.
No need, no use for armour.

A bullwhip, a quiver of arrows, a ray
gun less potent than a roadside bomb:
these would render the outlaws speechless,
the Sheriff of Nottingham livid, mute.

My heroes fed their secrets the raw
meat of righteous anger: parents
gunned down outside a theatre; an ambush
in Texas, left for dead among friends' corpses;
the haciendas of the heartless
rich; a false, venal brother usurping
the lion-hearted king's throne; the rebel
fleeing his broken army, thwarted country,
hunting any bountiful cause.

There could be irony, caustic wit,
Paladin quoting *Macbeth* to the mine owner
murdering prospectors for gold.
But no ambiguity. Ambivalence
resolved in a blaze of revelation
and gunfire. Selfless sidekicks
watched their backs, but no back-up
air power pounding their enemies' hide-outs.

No Kevlar helmets and vests,
no mangled limbs. Just a blood-soaked
shirt, a bandaged arm needing
a woman's soft hands,
and one night to heal. No aftershocks
of a brain concussed, no being
trapped in box canyons of memory
with migraines and gloom closing in.
Gun holstered, sword sheathed,
lips kissed, his eyes
scan again the horizon
of justice for the ultimately doomed
yet indispensable avatars of evil.

I'm crouched
behind the neighbour's hedge
with a trash can shield, broomstick spear,
water pistol with Amazon poison,
or curling iron converted to atomic zap.
Camouflaged
with lilac boughs, viscous red
ketchup smeared on my t-shirt, I'm ready
for the mortar shells of dirt clods falling,
the Luftwaffe revving inside a shed,
and, if needed, to dash to my home,
wake my grandmother, napping,
and carry her from the burning house.

HEROES: THE DRILL

When the school bell rings
one long, two short, take your coats
and proceed to the basement, single file.
This may or may not be a drill,
a time for prayers, for gratitude
that you were born, fed abundantly,
graced more or less with the leprechauns'
gold, and loved in all the major
and minor keys. This may be a prelude
to your first (of many) or your final
kisses. Lie down, face to the floor,
cover your heads with your coat,
so if the ceiling and rooms above
cave in, the debris will fall
on your legs, not your skulls.

Stop giggling. Bombs could be hurtling
down as I speak. No need to start
crying, either. You must be strong,
brave, prepared to find your parents
home, gawking at heartbreak
and hope on TV, or stumbling
dazed, searching for you in the long
rumbling and tremor.

But if the school bell rings on
and on, like an oven timer
when the roast is burning,
crawl under your desks, be turtles,
be Batman in his cave, imagine
the whimper of lions hurting
from the magic protecting your tent.
Think *tomorrow*. Make a fist
of steel around your heart.

All except Richard, you I can trust
to pull down the blinds against
breaking glass, heat sliding
like a ballplayer across home plate.
Keep your eyes closed, or else
your sight will melt, applause
heard through a thick, dark cloth
when the principal gives you the plaque
engraved for heroes with an eagle's face.

WHO TOLD YOU

I

Who told you I was a casualty
of peace, a veteran disabled
by pinball machines, a faulty
sense of when to leave the card table
and when to stop drinking? Who projected
on the screen of your boyhood thinking
the newsreel of unnerved me
and ex-GI buddies hell-bent
to close taverns down before slinking
into after-hour joints? Wives (mothers
like yours) no longer waiting for a cable
of regret. stop. in action. stop. Tethered
now to phone cords and strangling
the impulse to nag, fret, plead
please don't drive drunk.
The phone nonetheless dangling,
a woman screaming on and on,
marriage smashed by windshield
glass, your mother bleeding
into the crystal ball of your infant brain.

II

Before I died I leaned over your crib
and looked into the swirling milky
way behind your eyes, and saw the fibs
iridescent on your grandmother's feathery
tongue, how I was nearly slain
among the flotsam of Normandy, dropped
from a plane over Italy through snow and flak,
chased Rommel's tanks around the pyramids.
When what I did was the victory lap, help
mop up the D-Day aftermath, toss packs of
Camels to thankful tribes, chocolate bars
to the orphaned French, and roar my Jeep
past widows with rosaries, dressed in black.

And when your brain globe cleared, its zodiac
crowned with tales, your mother subtracted
to zero by electric shock and locked down
deep inside my death,
I was both miraculous
hero and hapless fool, a name on granite
under a plain white cross.

III

In your childhood bedroom you gazed
at two photos: Private Lemm, clean-shaven,
shining, yet unfazed by war, eyes
a haven for your longing to be lifted
where families might be grafted
together, all wounds of the flesh
and mind, healed. And Master
Sergeant H.M. Lemm, dark moustache,
skin ground down and blistered
by sleet, sun, sand, ash, smoke,
eyes remote, hard as gun metal, amazed
to be not dead. Glued
to the innocent portrait's back,
a poem, clipped from a yellowed newspaper:
All day and all night I dream
about you. The sea craves the shore
as I need you. And the stars
all night long spell your name.
Through that long bone marrow
fear, you, my son, were born.

IV

My death certificate says I was killed
on the way to be married. You were not told
that. Five men and one woman died
in my car. Your mother and I survived
the war, our love distilled

in a fetus. When you were nine months
we divorced. Up in flames
said your grandmother. The drive
to my second wedding arrived at a funeral.
As for the almost bride, *She was so pretty
and French and owned a café*,
your mother in her ancient kindly reveries
remembers, nursing home drugs abetting
this version of heartbreak
that haunted her into the madwomen's
ward, the diagnosis on her chart
that cost her so dearly, including
you. By the way, you (dis)appear
under "no descendents" of the deceased.
Yet I held you against my chest,
your breath on my veteran's
face, my bequest to you, orphan,
an old wound, mending, a purple heart.

SADDLEBAGS

I read somewhere that every generation
needs a war for its defining metaphor.
Mine was *Vietnam*. For my father's
father, too young to help
drive the last of the Sioux from Minnesota,
there was, later, *Spain,* its barbaric sun
flaring out and lighting his interior stage
with sugar-cane workers whipped bloody,
innocent women stripped naked, bodies
washed ashore from the battleship *Maine*
sunk off Cuba, the Hearst papers
blaming *Spain*. A false accusation, but
bold headlines spoke compellingly
to men like my grandfather reading
of *Spaniards* and *atrocities,*
enlisting to march through palm groves
in his dark blue metaphor of uniform.

What metaphors did he take
halfway around the world to Manila?
I have two. Matthias Lemm photographed
in his costume of war, brandishing six-guns.
A newspaper cartoon in that dénouement
year of imperial Spain and eve
of the *Yanqui* century: a bald-headed eagle
perched on a globe, one wingtip on Cuba,
one impaling the Philippines,
a hemisphere in its talons.
Like me, my grandfather was a carrier
of images. Were they virulent
as malaria, shrouded in flags,
brazen as bugles at dawn, lingering
rank as wounds in tropical rain?
Was that photo taken before or after
the sea voyage, the volleys, the corpses?

Was he feeling immortal, noble,
hair-brained, afraid? Could he foresee
his advance through coconut palms
leading deep into France, the Rhine,
the Mekong Delta, the Tigris-Euphrates?
Did he trade on the lustre of exploits,
on the skill of a midwife's hands
to the feet-first birth of his nation's
new power? Did he hide bloody
remembrance from his butcher-shop
clients and new wife in Dakota?
Or did he ride out, saddlebags heavy
with metaphors, and scatter those nuggets
in a prospector's played-out stream?

GRADE TEN WORLD HISTORY LESSON

Benjamin Franklin High School, Nov. 11, 1961

Take this down. America
rescued the world two
times. Tables were turning,
class, against the god-blessed
pursuit of happiness. Lacking our
firm purpose and might, our allies
twice lay crushed beneath the fallen
tree of liberty, and twice we seized
the axe from the enemies' hands.
We had no duty to make that noble
sacrifice, so many Americans dead, except
old friendships, love of freedom and
as the poet said, striving for Right.
Those warm-beer drinkers, those makers of
cheese and cathedrals and windmills and wine
would be shining their masters' boots
if we hadn't saved them. Rice-eaters and
tent-dwellers too, men married
to rickshaws and camels, women bent over
shrines and wells, if not for us,
they'd have nothing
but memories, or rumours, or fairy tales of
democracy.

*****

Proud, inspired, I wrote
(something like) this down:
America laced up its gloves, leapt
in the ring and KO'd the brutes in
both world wars! Once mighty
England reeling on the ropes, France
knocked cold in the early rounds,
the knee-buckling Dutch clutching the towel
and China's glass jaw shattered,
Sugar Ray America made mincemeat of
the enemy. The new and undisputed
heavyweight champion of the world.

*****

I knew almost everything then.
How Blue Angels and Thunderbirds
flashed across the beautiful and spacious
skies, wove contrails of glory.
How the brilliant general
turned genial commander-in-chief
made holes with his golf shoe spikes
in the White House floor the way his air force
left craters in Dresden and Hamburg.
I knew my grandfather Harry loved the other
plebeian Harry who famously said,
The buck stops here, and was ready
to back it up with the bomb. I knew
"The Battle of New Orleans" by heart,
and how many football fields could fit
on the deck of the Kitty Hawk where, once
I had earned my wings, I would lift off
with my squadron, close and lock
on Russian bombers, touch down
to sailors' cheers. Our nation's greatness
was everlasting like Paul Revere Ware
in my grandmother's kitchen –
and, if necessary, I'd ride all night,
over mountains and prairies, horse rearing,
hooves striking with terrible might.

I LIKED IKE (AND DICK, TOO)

for Kim Parker

This morning, dreaming, between
the conventions, the multi-coloured
Demos gone home, the white and right
folks, all god and guns, gearing up,
I was a guest in Dwight Eisenhower's
home. Bald, of course, his shiny face
smiling, he looked remarkably
well, for someone dead the year that Nixon
began to reign, and leaned across the dining table
as if seeking my support. Strap a helmet
on your head, I said, and you could lead
the troops into Germany, out of Iraq.
He just kept smiling.

My grandparents loved you, I said,
and Mother revered you like an aged
Achilles who'd survived Troy
to tell his grandchildren bedtime stories.
Most of us wore your campaign
buttons at school: *I like Ike
and Dick*. The latter meant nothing,
but the music of it worked, like
the click of a toy pistol's hammer
or the *tunk* of a good bunt laid down,
the echo of Dick Tracy more resonant
than Tricky Dick. Ike, however, meant
the Allies storming ashore on D-Day, brave
fathers home of their free will to sire *us*,
to show how mowers shave our evergreen
lawns, footballs soar above the democratic
turf, and every man (and woman) rules
the voting booth. Your opponent
was, we knew, a brilliant, dignified and
studious man, but what red-blooded kid
would root for an Adlai, an egghead.
Or my mother, who had prayed for you
to lead her husband through the fascist fire.

Your daughter served us tea and Fig Newtons.
To keep him regular, she said, and you kept
smiling. Remember how you left the Oval Office
floor, I said, riddled with a zillion holes
from your golf shoe spikes? From combat
boots to goofy clothes. Who didn't love
your grandfatherly face bent over
putting greens; the way, with stainless steel eyes
you leaned over maps of blood-drenched lines?
Few knew that behind your grin
was a mouth that sometimes exhaled gloom,
that warned against the "military-industrial
complex." When you wore brown suits
your staff knew to keep their distance.

Today, an orange shirt and yellow vest,
and I am in your hallway lifting up
your golf bag, setting it beside you,
but your daughter says, *He no longer plays,
can't remember how to swing… or other things.*
My beloved uncle golfed, I said, and voted
Republican. Two things I'd said that hell
would freeze over before I'd do. Well,
hell is halfway frozen now, I said,
but they don't make Republicans these days
like you, and Ike's smile grew wider.

One of your granddaughters spoke
at the Democrats' convention, an Eisenhower
for America's first black presidential
nominee. What do you think of that?
And it dawned on me that you had no idea
what I was saying, no idea of anything.

MY COUNTRY

1. Mercer Island

Tis of a creek
when I disobeyed my grandmother and rode
my bike across the floating bridge
the lake named for our father, Washington
to fish for trout
one small mile from the city's pounding heart,
that creek now surely tubed and stalled
beneath the software empire's building code,
the mall where trout paté,
farmed, flown in, is sold.

2. Anaheim

Sweet orange grove and clover land
where cousins herded their livestock
bees from orchards
and hives, now swarming with the traffic's
drone, honeyed music and brand
name outlets and security guards.

3. From the Mountains to Manhattan

The liberty to shoot the lone
grizzly, last rapids, the moon
posing over Manhattan, footage of the skyline
falling, the venal and valiant
alike, weeping, of thee I sing.

4. Sportsman's Tavern

I sing my grandfather's pride
in his tavern, crowning the good
Singapore Sling with a cherry, the ring
of cash registers bringing the fruited
plain to our table, a brotherhood
of bartenders defending the state

of their union, and customers who stood
beside Lou Gehrig battling, Elvis enlisting,
and Sugar Ray by a knockout in eight.

5. Lumberjack's Daughter

My grandmother shedding her grace
into canning jars, turkey stews, pie crusts
bulging with apples, knowledge she traced
to a logging camp, the civil liberties
of her parents' timber rights,
the majesty of cedars and Douglas firs
lifting her voice in a green canopy
of song that spread
across the years to my spacious skies.

6. Sweet

My country still bright with the foam
skimmed off a sea of shining words.
Bright with constellations beaming
new parables to the pilgrims
tracking light from above: one if by flood,
two if by heat. Bright with the glow
of casinos near the purple mountains,
amber waves in the palaces of sports,
coins littering the fountains,
blue veins transfused with faith
in the pursuit of a rainbow
trout in a creek once more flowing
and wearing away beneath
foundations of the sprawl and ascension
of home

FOOTNOTE FOR THE INCIDENT IN THE POTOMAC

The hurricane has levelled a city.
The waters have ruptured the dikes,
flooded the coast, blown apart
underwater cages at a naval base
and the forcibly conscripted dolphins
have escaped, armed and dangerous.

Out there in the Gulf of Mexico
and cruising the Caribbean islands,
laser-guided missiles strapped to their hulls,
nicknamed Top Gun, Finny the Kid,
Deadeye Jeddi, Bonnie, and Clyde,
they're searching for terrorist frogmen.

So far, no scuba divers at a Cuban resort
have been blasted to bits, no coral reef
photographers. No startling apparitions for marine
biologists, no archaeologists taking cover
inside sunken ships. No dolphin-loving
tourists blown up in sightseeing boats.

*American pilots are target practicing
on water buffalo in Vietnam*, said Tony
my prof in American Lit. Our text was Mailer,
Why We Are in Vietnam. Tony slammed
his hand on the table, hard: *You don't
mess with the water buffalo god.*

You just don't mess.

EULOGY FOR A DRAFT BOARD

for J.C.

Praise to the charcoal men
who sat, deaf oracles, in a drywalled
temple of justice, nailing
my conscientious youth with objections:

What would you do if a vicious gang
assaults your girlfriend on a night-dark street
intent on rape, and you
a pacifist, you refuse to fight?

I would smash their faces with a trash can
lid, their skulls with a brick, bite,
kick their balls through the uprights
like the final, triumphant play of the season.

What if soldiers, Chinese or Russian,
burst into your home and start shooting?
Will you quote Ghandi, try to reason
with Kalashnikovs? Will you dispute,

like some Socrates, with Soviet tanks?
I would bow humbly, offer them drinks,
hum "Lara's Theme," quote the *I Ching*
and lob grenades of Homeric thanks

at the White House, Imperial Palace, the Kremlin.
Praise to the unsmiling cinder block men
who found sufficient cracks in my pipe dream
of peace to rule me fit for saluting

with an M-16 the palm trees, elephant grass,
rice paddies teeming with gremlins.
Thanks to you, now long dead, I voted
with my feet, to a north-of-y'all address.

Down south, this year, a high school teammate,
wounded in Nam, tells me over rum and Coke,
he's warned his sons he'll take his baseball bat
and break their legs if they're sent to Iraq.

Seattle, 1965 / 2007

I'LL BE GONE

for Jef Jaisun

On a warm autumn night in Seattle,
moving from one embrace to another
at my fortieth high school reunion
in the grand ballroom of the Lincoln Hotel
one month before the US elections
with news of daily blasts in Iraq growing fainter,
I'm pulled aside, gently, in front of a giant mirror
in which I see the survivors, laughing, resuming the dance
and am told, in a soft voice I must lean over and strain
to hear, *Your high school sweetheart and first
wife is listed among the deceased.*

The next to last time
I saw her, dancing and laughing
around a bonfire, we were the guests of honour –
a warm autumn night, a beach near Seattle,
gallons of Gallo wine, Steve thrumming his guitar,
yours truly on bongos, people shouting out Dylan's
"Don't Think Twice, It's All Right," we were
crossing the northern border, next day, immigrant
cards in our wallets, draft notice
returned to sender. She was flaunting
her half-naked body, hugging whoever
stayed awake, wrapped in a moonlight blanket
at the water's edge. For every face but mine,
her gaze melted sealing wax on letters goodbye.
I stared forlornly at this shoreline
I might never see again, while she could
glide back home and frolic, here, anytime,
with anyone. Then Steve
sat beside me, close to the embers,
waiting for my eyes to open
on the pink-gray dawn sky.
She's gone, he said, *left your backpack but took
your car, heading back to California,
loves you but all she could see*

to the north was white. Blanc. No lights
of the Golden Gate, no eucalypt-scented
sex under the palm-treed stars, no
dance of deliverance from the rockets' red
glare, no sweet kickass prayers
of the Grateful Dead or Thomas Jefferson
airplane in which rebels could soar, just

frost. The last time I saw her, the same
year Steve went missing in action
in the jungles of Nam, she found her way
north of the border, migrant bohemian
fruit-picker under Okanagan skies
and blistering sun. Out of the blue
she dropped by my Vancouver beach house,
tripping on acid with her marble-David-look-alike
boyfriend whose parents owned that Big Sur
café where the Beats set their poems
on fire and lobbed them at the air-conditioned
post-war dream. The day so clear
the white arrowheads of the Olympic
Mountains in Washington gleamed beyond
the Strait of Juan de Fuca's invisible border.
Remember, I thought, those alpine
meadows and streams, the two of us, zip-together
sleeping bags, chocolate, tequila, reading
Walt Whitman, *I sing the body electric*, gathering
blossoms like Whitman with his flower press
in the troop camps and battlegrounds
of a blue-gray war. I fought
with myself that day to be civil, gracious
host. How could you show up without
warning, stoned, entwined with this
demigod male I could never be?
Unsaid. Smiled, made up the guest bed.
Woke the next morning to find them
gone. A note. *Thank you for
your kindness. Don't forget
to look up "in perfect silence at the stars."*

No word, no news, since. Until
this evening, when a classmate tells me
his son's stationed in Iraq, and he wishes
he'd gone to Canada years ago, like me.
Was it rough, he asks, leaving like that?
Only at first, I say. And now.

THE QUAY OF REGRET

I could have sailed to Saigon.
Mr. Jackson, merchant marine
and father to my friend Jerome, is home
on leave, drinking Jamaican rum,
spinning platters for his boys: heartsick
Otis Redding on his San Francisco dock,
Willie Dixon lamenting, "I Can't Quit
You, Baby," and Junior Wells growling out,
through clenched teeth, "Vietcong Blues."

Jerome, restless, sarcastic, needs his mojo
working, wants James Brown, has no
respect for his old man, wants to bolt
outside for a joint with our wilder friends,
nookie with Carlotta, his future of hoisting
TVs and stereos through unlatched windows.
Here's a life for you Lemmy baby,
Mr. Jackson says, placing on the turntable
Ray Charles' first single, from Ray's Seattle years

a long way from home, from Nat Cole
imitations in Florida clubs and bars.
*He began to find what he had to say
and how to say it, here, but you ain't
seeing eye to eye with yourself yet.
I can get you a seaman's ticket, just like that.*
So many freighters to Nam, and so few guys
signing up, even for the danger pay,
leery of mines in the harbour, cargo delays,

being stuck for weeks in Saigon now teeming
with hustlers, hookers, thugs, assassins.
I had been reading Conrad, *Lord Jim*,
fancied my shipshape self in the monstrous
prose and shimmering poetry of the sea,
scraping paint, tightening bolts, oiling
valves and winches to earn my passage.
Drinking in dockside bars with anchor-strong
men, women with the world on their tongues,

more real and exotic than anthropology
class which I'd stopped attending. Would-be
writers need to survive, and book jackets
back then still said *worked as a deck hand,
bartender, railroad brakeman and*
what better way than freighters and Asian ports?
But *I can't do that*, I hear myself say, forty
years later, *I'm opposed to the war, can't help
ship supplies, though otherwise....* I gulp

back my ambivalence, mumble my downcast
gratitude, my noble idiotic morality
drowning the second-guessing, the risk-taking
romance going under once, twice,
a righteous, joyless third time. I look at the face
of Jerome, studying the laces of his football
all this while, that dream he once stroked
of being the next Jim Brown, before the tokes,
the spread-open legs of girls, cheap wine

from the Chinese corner store. In Taiwan
decades later, my other self, who said *for sure*
to Mr. Jackson, goes ashore, nurses beer
after beer, cogitates on the blur
of voices in the quay of regret, the whoop
and wharf where the flotsam of history slap
against one another. I wave off the red-lipped
women, not in the mood tonight, the news
from an old classmate back home, blues

for Jerome, dropped dead at fifty-seven,
cause unknown. Back in my bunk, driven
toward the rocks by wave after wave of faces
I might have transfixed with glowing words,
if I had said to Mr. Jackson, *Not now. No.*

RICHARD SPEAKS TO ME, THE FAINT-HEARTED

You do not understand Crusades.
First, the clothes, the finest velvets,
damasks, brocades, dyed with sunsets
and woven from the swallow's flight.
And the star-bright, sky-curved
armour, voluptuous and blinding
enough for archangels facing Lucifer.
Never underestimate the glamorous
grace of a cruciform hilt in a scabbard,
the thrill of a full heart racing
on horseback, under chain mail.
Yes, the horse, which will magnificently
die beneath you, God giving
His creatures to bear forth our glory.

You know nothing now but celluloid
gore, guts strewn, groans, and carrion
birds feeding. Heroes, briefly
rueful, search for fallen comrades
before, in closing scenes, vassals cheer
their shining king, and you leave the theatre,
smiling. But I walked among the dead,
declaring, *Dear thee in heaven* and *thou art
in hell*. Convinced our vanquished foes
had swallowed their gems and gold,
I had three thousand stomachs
cut open. My men took great pleasure
in kicking their severed heads.
You deny, you mock
the weight of sin, which we bore
like arrowheads, sunk deep, shafts
broken off, flesh scarred over.

If everything you regret, all your remorse,
your fear of damnation, could be drained
with your blood by blade or bomb
and you awake, absolved, in paradise,
would you not seek my kind of death?
Then, too, the enemy, the value of
which you take far too lightly.
Infidels and their perfidy acquit
almost anything: sending foot soldiers
up siege ladders, mounting
and draining oneself into unblemished
boys' bodies and soon-to-be corpses
of women, honouring the Holy Father's
command to turn their towns into candelabras,
mosques into stables. You are righteous
and have come this far,
at such expense, in so much peril,
to defend the kingdom
from unholy dung,
from thieves
who have stolen God's name,
from hashish-eating, black-cloaked
Assassins whose eyes are ruthless
with hatred for the majesty
and salvation of my sword.

PATRIOTS

PATRIOTS I: LOOKING UP, LOOKING DOWN

A spectral man in an Irish-knit sweater
walks past the White House
twice each day, always looking up,
angled at whatever the sky's illuminated
manuscript writes back to him,
expression sort of bemused, but mostly
ethereal. He never stumbles or strays
off the curb into the linear
flow of the century. Oncoming
pedestrians sidestep or veer.
Eyes assigned to track and target
unhinged intentions have long since
removed him from their scope.
He is all vision beneath a brown tweed cap,
the kind I bought in Ireland nine months
after a bomb performed caesarean
sections on British soldiers
in a Birmingham pub, and two days after
Éamon de Valera, first president of the Republic
died. I was learning
a Vivaldi concerto on my alto recorder
in a Trinity College classroom
overlooking the Dublin street where de Valera's
funeral procession was almost underway.
Éamon dipped his fingers in Irish blood
to help paint the love cries
of revolution on Dublin's walls.
Vivaldi influenced O'Carolan,
a Trinity music prof told me, Ireland's blind
composer and poet, a harpist plucking dazzling
feathers from angels, stuffing the goose
of Irish folksong with Italian Baroque dressing.
Two policemen entered the room
just as I'd finally subdued a troublesome
arpeggio. Politely, but with a voice
like a stone mason's chisel, one asked me
to leave, and while I packed my scores
and recorder, the other assembled a tripod,

a high-powered rifle with scope.
Someone might try to assassinate the president's
corpse? I almost asked. Precautions,

the sharpshooter said, his colleagues
stationed along the route looking down
on the innocent, hapless and incendiary
bystanders of heightened moments in history,
the fireworks, the passing of messiahs,
O'Carolyn's Dream, his Ode to Whiskey,
his Lament. A widow in a clothing shop in Union Hall,
County Cork, sold me my cap and told me
the pattern of every Aran Isle sweater is unique
so the drowned bodies of fishermen can be
identified. The gaunt man looking up
recognizes what design? A helicopter
ascending from the mansion's chopper pad?
Contrails blurring like the voices of Irish
and Italian immigrants in the fields and streets?
Flag-draped coffins or bodies washing ashore
with the clouds? Buxom milkmaids and slouching beasts?
The shape of a country where all gentle
desires rule? Only the brim of his cap?
Mine was stolen in an artists' colony pub.
I cannot hear Vivaldi without looking
up at one Trinity College window while
a father of Irish independence, emptied now
of luck, charm, guile, conciliation,
ruthlessness and devotion, rolls by.

PATRIOTS II: SOFTENING

She was a paper pusher, processing prisoners. After hours, she would drop in to visit her boyfriend...who was one of the night guards. It was the night guards' job...to 'set the conditions' for military interrogation by softening the prisoners up. [She] was happy to help her boyfriend out.
— Margaret Wente, *The Globe and Mail*, May 8, 2004

Sin is putting someone in a position they're not prepared for.
— John Corr (in Dr. Robert J. Grimm, *Neurology Works*)

The prisoners had moustaches, like so many men
back home, my softball coach, volunteer
firemen, security guards at shopping malls,
Magnum PI. But those men didn't pray
lying down, didn't mind one bit stripping
shirts off at the lake, after victory or a tough
defeat, or training hoses on charred
smoking walls, or a day of false alarms
or night shifts all alone arrested
by the window display in a lingerie store.
The prisoners' skin, not magnolia,
but the desert at dusk or the green brown
sea beneath my eyelids
in the warm night wind.

Like all prisoners everywhere they
claimed to be innocent
bystanders, outraged or devastated
victims, but how could you tell
satellite TV installers from snipers,
car thieves from suicide bombers,
protestors who want their saviours
gone from patriots who want us
dead? Only those acting suspicious
get picked up, and if they're nabbed
they must've been doing something
wrong. And wrong here rhymes with
up-to-no-fucking-good which means
terrorism back home. The real problem,

said one sergeant, is they're animals,
whimpering at the feet of whatever
dude's insane and smart enough
to cut so many throats he gets to
be dictator, then they snarl
at us when we try to free them.

Soften them up, we, the lowly
guards, the paper pushers, were told
by those wipe-my-ass interrogators
from OGA, *fuck a PUC* whenever you want
to vent your frustration and *set the conditions*
for the vital-for-national-security
work they do. And that softening
which we were commended for, and was us
just fooling around, and done in sport,
which didn't go too far, looked funnier than
hell, so pictures were taken. Everyone
saw them. Man, didn't you
ever yank someone's pants down?
Take a Polaroid of somebody passed out
head in the john at a party? blindfold
new teammates and make them stick their hands
in a bucket of slime or walk around the locker room
in the opposite sex's underwear?

Then some candy-ass do-gooder complained,
and next thing you'd think we'd been ripping out
toenails or burning some guy's balls
with smokes. Like, these people take their enemies'
heads off. With swords. They're high
explosives, and we were supposed to
defuse them.

What did our genius leaders
think? We wouldn't exercise freedom
to use the cameras, computers, internet
we were fighting for? And how come

bleeding hearts back home were shocked
by a pile of live, naked bodies.
A patriot's soft-core
porn. Hands tied
behind their backs, standard
procedure, everywhere. But not
a leash around their necks?
All I said was, *Look, he's hard*,
and grinned. What's wrong
with smiling? With following orders
to soften them up? And now so much is
hardening against me, and all the good I did
and didn't sign up to do.

OGA stands for "Other Governmental Agencies," e.g., the CIA

PUC refers to "Person Under Control"; to "fuck a PUC" meant to beat a detainee

FIVE THINGS DISGUSTED HIM

After Anna Akhmatova's "Three Things Enchanted Him"

He's the most ruthless man I ever met. And I mean that as a compliment.
— Henry Kissinger on Donald Rumsfeld, US Secretary of Defence
Quoted in *The Globe and Mail*, May 8, 2004

Grown-ups
who patted him on the head,
their hands worse than cobwebs
threading the dimly lit shed
or earwigs in the laundry tub.

Teachers who said he was wrong,
their skulls thick as cast-iron kettles,
eyes roaming like blackboard erasers.
the cold spaghetti of their brains,
dry rot in their hearts' aimless hulls.

Later, the fools
with star-studded shoulders, afraid
men would die on their watch.
He would provide them
with balls, tattoo his orders on the back

of their hands: where to aim, when to fire.
The pundits, those dilettantes who dispatch
limp epistles from their keyboard crutch.
Those philanderers of history who conspire
behind the drapes. For them, he is no Hamlet

but Hamlet's knife, prying the plot
from the playwrights, their reluctance
to make words polar enough to freeze
the truth, a glacier on the enemy's camps,
sealing, unflinching, his gaze.

HENDRIX OF ARABIA

Rainbow scarves, peacock shirt, gypsy
trousers, Robin Hood boots – he is all mirage
at first, spotted by a convoy on a sweltering road
near Basra, a purple haze from refineries
behind him. A gang of kids, jaws unhinged,
drop the rocks they were aiming
when that detonation of
hair, that face like feedback from a space
station imploding, those trigger fingers on
his Stratocaster, come into view.
Here there is one god, one prophet, or now
maybe two. A fury of chords
catches fire and the kids
are idolaters – the words for martyr,
roadside bomb and vengeance
cauterized from their brains.
The convoy halts. Marines, voodoo
children of their star-spangled
parents who once were stoned
on his machine gun smoking
the beehives of the planet. He hums
and honey flows from their calibred
barrels. This is not what they signed
up for. To escort him, riding
shotgun, north, past the watchtower
mosques, men's heads turning,
incandescent, toward the northwest
Pacific coast, past women
in the foxholes of their veils
remembering how the desert wind
dries the most sacred names to dust.
He is driving a Jeep into Baghdad
through the legions' armor, cellphones
ringing with resignations
from pentagons and oval offices, the blood
red house of the sky
low enough to kiss.

TO CASTRO ON HIS 80ᵀᴴ BIRTHDAY

Now, the one reliable assassin
draws near. No five-hour speech
will pacify or instruct him
in revolutionary protocol. Beachheads
of tourists infiltrate the workers'
consciousness, their lifetimes of being
reverent and grateful to their saviour,
their wish list modest, but growing.
So long ago, it seems, the juntas
and their *Yanqui* amigos built firewalls
against the Cuban virus. But the code
of self-assertion, more in the long haul
threatening, spreads. Up the road

the ninth president since Jack
took that puzzling bullet in the neck
rides toward his sunset, aims his ersatz
version of an Eastwood sneer at detractors,
his skull alas poorly suited for Stetsons
the real Texan in the White House wore
when El Presidente still shot
hoops, hugged Russians, a loose
cannon in our hemisphere. One more
lame duck, feathers unruffled, struts
self-assured toward his legacy, eggs
in one charred basket. Strength gutted,

gaunt, the visionary on his long, last legs,
he watches his latest, meagre nemesis
on CNN *Español*, that brave-face gesture
from Air Force One, while the plazas
and boulevards of the new and ancient worlds
swarm, in his dimming eyes, with his unfurled
prophecies, a billion raised fists of the masses.

Cayo de Coco, 2006

IN THE BEGINNING

Words, the tongue's bright needles
flush with adrenaline vowels,
blood-doping syllables, plosives injected
through the ears, fricatives that prick
the eyes, volatile labials pooling
where the synapses ignite, and inkjet
diphthongs direct to gut
and groin. Words that copulate
with fear, words like a voyeur's
binoculars trained on the stripped bare
intentions of those framed
in the window of opportunity, consumed,
unbalanced by unholy chimerical terror.
Words to pull the trigger
of endorphins when the elected,
locked on the target, bring us good cheer.

Mundane words, functional as a leash
for walking the dog, as toilets or glue,
are struck by lightning, fused together, and glow
with an oracle's fire: 9/11.
You see those clouds rise to a heaven
contested by martyrs, by victims; a threshold
of rubble we cross to hear the prophets
name the transfigured world, intone
mantras to breathe in hope, breathe out
wrath, to elevate our voices
in the anthem's flourish and its drone.

New words, mutations, by-products of good
intentions fertilized with deadly sins:
Taliban, its echo of Prospero's need
to enslave the savage for his lofty ends;
of dark tribes with barbaric codes,
drinking from skulls;
or alien inhabitants of a planet
governed by principles of pain.

And old, enduring words: shadows
from their black wings stilling songbirds
in meadows and wood; wind off the glaciers
freezing flowers, the fruit in bud.
Words with the stare of Medusa.
Words, the indelible stain of blood.
That save; that savage.
One side of the world, *America*
eclipses the sun,
floods the world with mirrors and smoke;
the other, *Muslims* mar
the moonlight sonata
with their crude music.
Words like hot irons branding.
Words that are tabernacles
of freedom and safety, chambers
of shackles and horror. Open, see
the hallowed treasure
briefly, before the blinding.

AGAIN, THE PSALM

Shamaa, Lebanon, Aug. 21 (2006) – Israeli soldiers in the hilltops watch as Hezbollah men on dirt bikes patrol the valleys, barely a mile away.
  – New York Times

Again, the psalm is the shadow
of death, the valley home
by perilous home now churning
with splintered beds and bones
and molecules of wasted
atonement.

Once more, the voices blaming,
claiming greater grievances.
Who has least tasted honey and milk.
Who this time was first to render
flesh into martyrs, wives
into widows. Clouds of grief

billow where god's name is
relentlessly spoken. We crave still
waters, all factions cry, merciful
meetings in orange and olive groves,
a sky blessed with jet planes
full of tourists and pilgrims.

Again the roads are choked
with righteousness camouflaged
as tanks, as rockets launching
families into the safety of oblivion.
O lord, all implore, drive the thief
from our wells, our table, anoint

our heads bowed to the holiness of loss,
uplifted to the sirens of heaven.

WASTED BREATH

Forget about the suffering of others
far away, you have no room.
Turn off news about people fleeing
volcanoes or drought-plagued villages
for the smothering slums, ignorant
armies of freedom and pillage.

You have plenty here to fret
and fume about – a sex offender
in the neighbourhood, taxes collected
for another stadium, sidewalk vendors
of highs and lows, the nicely groomed
articulate terrorist next door.

Remember those countless hours spent
staring at the wounded on the screen
or reading experts on a conflict's origins?
Have you stopped any tanks in their tracks,
steered the animals onto an ark, cried
in a voice, distilled from those clips and bites,

so strong that eardrums of the apathetic bleed?
Who would sacrifice the choice
cuts of meat, timber turned into pianos
sounding all the dissonance and harmony of love
and faith? Not I, saving my next breath
for you, my friend.

AIRSPACE

When you listen, dumbfounded,
to suave grave men
and women who lie
about war, you're a bird
sucked into a jet engine.
You're not even a brief flash
of iridescence on their screens.
You try, like most, to fly
below the radar, saying, *I can't afford*
more than briefly to care
what's below the Glorious People's dam,
who ate black and white alphabets
until their tongues turned grey,
where food shipments mystically went,
who bombed the refugee camp,
what the phoenix of resuscitation theory
sets on fire when reborn.
But the radar finds you
anyhow. The chameleons of
investments know that lies
launch all great ships, honesty
wrecks on the coastline
of our smug or regretful indifference.
Look, the wordslingers glide
across the lobby toward you,
all smiles or scowls, depending –
disguised as party faithful, as secretaries
of the state of perpetual triumph and fear.
Too late, you hear
the afterburners, roaring.

BOATMEN OF ARBEIA

A Roman document from about AD 400 called the Notitia Dignitatum *– a list of all the military and civil posts of the empire – refers to an irregular unit of "bargemen from the Tigris," based at Arbeia, the fort nearest modern South Shields [England].*
— Charlotte Higgins, "When Iraqi Peacekeepers Stood at Hadrian's Wall," *The Guardian Weekly*

The cold is different here, dank
and putrid like the offal of an animal
even vultures neglect.
The sun appears, but refuses
to kiss our hands, their frigid
grip around our oars. The throats of
the legionnaires, when not spewing
bravado and glory, choke with curses;
unable to wake
from this dream of empire
pushing ever outward, a catapult
flinging them from vineyards in Gaul
or promises of villas in Hispania,
against this wall, the Pictii with their coastal
raids and hunting dogs howling,
the rotting breath of the estuary,
and the wind's white fur.

And us, the Tigris boatmen,
dredged from our sweltering marshes
or plucked from cataracts spilling
down Anatolian mountains, hauled across deserts
and a lapus lazuli hallucination of sea,
the vast chorus of dark green
voices lining the shores.

Barates, our Syrian brother, a merchant,
berates us when, soured by the Britons'
execrable ale, or buoyed by a cask
of tolerable wine, we float back
like white storks over marshlands
or hawks in the gorges above those rapids

we mastered, to our hills of ash groves,
pistachios, oaks, the fragrance
of *sikbaj*, beef stewing in dill, coriander,
vinegar and honey. Fattened by
selling silk flags and standards to soldiers,
flaunting Regina, the Kentish slave he freed
and married, he boasts of the Syrian archers
guarding the wall, their altar to Baalbeck,
the shrine to Astarte where he prayed
for Regina's fertility. Erect
as the temple of Isis in London, he spouts
paeans to his kingdom, older than Rome,
rising from the grouse nests and gorse,
bogs and mutton-bone dumps.

How one's triumphs may be rewarded
with exile. With gloom.
Our doom was to skilfully guard Rome's
eastern frontier at Fluvium Tigram, where
the Mediterranean road met our river
and the thrust of the Persian threat.

We should be proud to be chosen
to defend the river's mouth against pirates
and barbarians, and in uneventful hours
to ferry olives, dates, quern-stones
and glassware, pheasants and oysters
for this monumental outpost of Imperium.
And I confess to imagining, when the north
wind sheathes its sword and I climb
the wall with Barates and a Roman engineer,
my children's children paying homage
to their ancestors' mother goddess and
to me, at my grave among the sheep and corn.
And to extravagant, ruthless, meticulous
genius, this triumph of architects and armour,
motley gods and emperor cults, procurators
of mines and granaries, and the net flung
wide as the world, snaring simple boatmen.

CHONGCHON / SAIGON / BAGHDAD

To be defeated is to know
the infinite light trapped in darkness

to be blessed by sailors with sharks'
pure smiles, aboard ships on the ocean's floor

to hear the bone songs of horses
scattered on the red-rivered plain

is to dance on moss thick as flamencos
to the forest's guitars, with gypsy ghosts.

To be twice defeated is to plunge
from a mountain rampart

and shatter in a chandelier concerto
among the desert's obsidian jewelry

to be volcano no longer. To bow
and withdraw thrice in a lifetime

trinity of unhallowed retreats, is to see
without looking the jungle grow back

sand drift and thicken over the barracks
the monuments erected by one's enemy

obliterate all evidence of grandeur
is to breathe golden spores of a wind

holier than the sun's raw tongue, a wind
from a sky now purged of needful gods

is to dance as the sea dances
to the moon's carnal, insouciant music

is to crave one's own blood and no other's.
To know defeat is to crawl

inside the labyrinthine ear of the earth
and hear what the aquifers are saying:

there is no dignity, no pride to be
restored, in dying beside the wells.

There is thirst, and thirst quenched only
when everyone drinks, fused with forbearance.

RETRIBUTION

Hannibal's favourite elephant
hates the snow, the wind's icy needles
piercing his ears, the white howl
smothering the sky. This is not what
he crossed that vast undrinkable
turquoise pool to endure.
Tricked into believing he was
royalty, as elephants should be, rowed
by men across the sea, men
working the sails, men dropping
from exhaustion, straining to show
the elephants a landscape majestic
as them. You are mountainous,
said Hannibal, flattering him
onto the barge, at last
you will walk atop a world
worthy of you. Hannibal's favourite
elephant longs for the black
volcanic glass of the desert.
Hears the flat, cracked, bugling
notes of an elephant's soul
vanishing before its time. Sees
in the swirling snow the flocks of
egrets that escort the soul away.
He knows, too, the elephant gods
are not amused. Hannibal lied.
The gods will deny him
Rome, will roar in Caesar's ear
their demand that Carthage be smashed,
its rubble scattered across the sands.
That Hannibal's name be remembered
as a synonym for grandiose
failure, and elephant
ghosts in the snow.

THE TRUE MEANING OF HONOUR

After his latest accident at a jousting tournament, his wife
left with his horse, trailer and pick-up truck.

Except for the instruments of his ears
and his sternum, he has broken
every bone in his body. His home
town's biology teacher wants his skeleton
for the classroom, a sailor's scrimshaw
or Inuit's inscribing of fracture lines.

His horse, Charlemagne, an Appaloosa
gelding, was last seen beneath him
at the Amateur Jousting Club of Maryland.
He swore by that old cavalry adage
adopted last year by the Order of the Boar
jousters of New Zealand: first the horse,
then the gear, then the man. The man
lavished so much love on Charlemagne,
his wife's position now is somewhere between
Baltimore and Butte, behind the wheel
of the truck she chauffeured all those years of
slings, casts, strapped ribs and shoulders –
Charlemagne's horsey dreams, in the trailer,
of the Dragon's Lair Jousting Festival
in Orangeville, or New Riders of the Golden Age
at War Horse Farm in Florida.

Legs encased in plaster and elevated
in a hospital bed, he knows nothing
of his wife's flight to freedom.
The *joust à plaisir* had ceased to please her.
Too absorbed with his horse's caparisons
to notice his wife
wanted finery, too, wanted heralding
and uncourtly love, had grown tired
of being a lady in waiting.
But the weight of the lance
lowered at full gallop

balances the brain behind his visored eyes
the way the grail of his wife's or any woman's body
never could, not even Vinrac's, the rebel maiden
from Warwick Castle's Devil's Horsemen.
Even the fall from Charlemagne,
after a green knight's masterful blow, left him
stunned with gladness, gazing at a sky
free of the pennants of debt and drudgery
at a cubicle's computer screen back home.
And when the lists of sales accounts
dissolve into the lists of combat,
he swears fealty to an older, deeper code
and rises in the stirrups, salutes the court
as he now, in traction, points the remote
toward the History Channel, searching
the true meaning of honour.

THE PYRAMIDS

I observe the ones who apologize
for nothing, or wrap our complaints
in the soft fur of their groomed regrets.
They are the founders
of cities where glaciers recede,
the seers that divine
the aquifers from nomads' wells,
the synapses that make light
flow from the primal spark to empire's grid.
Or so they would have us believe,
filling the air with their fragrance,
demure as divas when they bow,
their bodyguards saving them seats
in history's limousine.

How they refuse the gift
of guilt, leave that space in their brain
for compassion open like a coffin lid.
Dressed in the dark
clothes of denial, they lose sleep
over failures to thrust
to steer their brilliance past their rivals
on hairpin curves. Crash
and it's the other driver's fault.
Acquitted of their luxuries and guile,
sipping cheap champagne, I bathe daily
in modest good fortune, and blame
the gold mines' tailings, the stockpiles
of fission and fusion, the buffalo's absence
on an atavistic fang in their DNA.
Merely one of countless middlemen,
I tally the great stones dragged
to the pyramids, the bodies
crushed and spirited away.

WHAT I WANTED TO BE

ANNUNCIATION

After Jeremy Smith's silkscreen print "Distant Searchlights"

I

You have seen this landscape before.
One night inside your mother – driving
away from the rest of her
life, high on the interior's
gravity, she stopped her car
and walked toward the clouds
convulsed by a rising moon.
Before that, in Holland, through the eyes
your father wore, walking ahead
of his platoon, scanning for snipers'
hide-outs. In your dream
with just the lamppost to hide behind.
Or after you read Louis L'Amour,
your wrists tied with wet leather thongs
to the posts, war cries of dreaded
Apaches dwindling toward the horizon
where the sun, soothing you with lavender,
unsheathed its knife. Once you camped
down a back road in Arizona and woke to the howls
of drunken cowboys coming to cut your throat –
coyotes, in fact, drawing so close they stole
your eyes and left you theirs and this landscape
with the lights of Phoenix encroaching.

II

You wanted to be James Dean leaning
against that lamppost, or one of Bogart's women.
All the Miles Davis kinds of blue
rolling and cresting across the ancient inland sea.
A hitchhiker on that Montana highway
picked up by a luminous omnisexual soul-
fusing traveller from the Large Magellanic Cloud.
Amelia Earhart seeing the searchlights of home

and flying on, into mystery. Not you, trying
to hook your fingers into clefts of light
to pry back the great blue whale clouds.
More often lured by the profane attraction
those searchlights annunciate.

III

You are a child, a product, a photon
and emissary of those distant
lights, but the lamppost in the middle of
Nowhere and Everywhere is your spinal cord
and brain, signals firing
your life like a shell exploding where no one
but coyotes will find you. Or a fire
signalling to a mother racing
beyond her life, a father about to step
on a landmine. The luminous sign of
release for the captives
who've scaled the walls and are running
to meet you. On the road so long,
you can't tell dusk from dawn,
and pull the car off the road
to rest, hear Ellington's "Mood Indigo,"
make love to her in the backseat, and listen
for nighthawks or meadow larks. Any moment
the searchlights may swing down on your face
or shut off. Out there, in a grey-blue furrow,
an animal with your eyes is
talking with something
you call god.

WHAT I WANTED TO BE

A dandelion and buttercup bouquet
on grandmother's vanity, the wasps
in the pears, the long white
jet plane's tail in the blue-eyed
Sunday school Jesus sky, a cavalry
bugle, anyone with spurs on a palomino, a nurse
before my best friend called me a sissy.

Safe from basements, from closets, from the emptiness
of grandfather's bottle of whiskey.
Dr. Chesley's hand on my forehead's
Sahara. A voodoo doctor's blood-red
breath sucking pins from my mother's brain
until she acts normal again.

Second chair clarinet till I die
next to first clarinet Janet Dupree.
The brave Marine who caught the live
grenade and threw it back at the Russians
when they tried to storm our neighbourhood.
The monks who make my Anglican
church's concord grape communion wine.

A priest who could talk directly to god.
A home run king with a crown
that would make Grandfather smile.
Great-grandmother at ninety-nine, never scared
of mice in her attic, of the dark trail
to her outhouse, of the rats in the blackberry
patch where we filled and filled our pail.

A silver bullet, deep in the chest
of the drunk driver who laid
my father to rest. The brown-sleeved
arm of St. Francis lined with birds.
The ball about to be blessed
by Willie Mays' outstretched glove.

Great Uncle Walter who got winged
in a lumberjacks' feud yet still chopped down
giant cedars with his arm in a sling.
Benny Goodman coming to town
to swing so hot my grandma in her hospital bed
would rise, don her pearls, mink coat and heels,
twirling to an encore that never ends.

TRAIL

I

I ran away first from Boston
with Great-grandma, from overstuffed
parlours and women's downcast
knitting gazes, from merchant men grooming
moustaches and sons. Sat upright and
brave on the wagon I coloured
on my stretch of the Westward Ho! mural
blazing around Miss Cooper's classroom walls,
Great-grandma striding ahead of her mules
toward the west coast forests of Washington.

Fled with the great horned owls
from my great-uncles' tug-of-war
on their buck saw, the back-broken
firs and cedars falling in the coastal fog,
Great-grandma tending the bush fires
that cleared the way for the songbirds.

I glided one wide-eyed-moon night
from her lumberjack camp without her
blessing, airborne on rumours of
soaring over France, creased leather and
faces, Grandpa swooping us low
over bogged-down enemy troops
while I leaned out, scarf trailing
like Snoopy's, and dropped bombs with deadly
playground accuracy on classmates
whose turn it was to play German.

And long before that I fled
the cross-fire of the Reformation
with ancestors in Holland who high-tailed it
to the Lower Rhine, turned into sausage makers
and Germans. Then, tired of entertaining
and evading mercenary gangs of soldiers
looking for action after Napoleon's war,
I leapt for a boat with Heinrich, Maria and
eight children landing in buffalo country,
where settling and escaping felt the same.

II

Packed a pillowcase with cookies and clothes
one twelve-year-old night and ran away
from the screaming, the coppery reek of bourbon,
the whiskey glass I'd bought him for Christmas
smashing on the table I'd made for her in wood shop,
shouted at the door: *I'm leaving and never
coming back* to her *Never should've married
you in the first place* and his *I could drop
dead tomorrow then who'd look after you and
the kid*. I hid myself under the porch for hours,
house falling silent, lights going
out, front door locking.

Flung myself into baseball, football, even track
where I could run, evade, pursue,
leave the old gouged desks and the teachers'
transfusing stares of ambition, slog
through mud for a few yards forward,
chop a behemoth down, sense the footfalls
of other runners growing fainter behind me,
float toward the outfield fence,
slide safely home.

And when those triumphs failed,
I found myself waiting
inside an ancient great-grandmother's
parlour, stuffed with books
I'd read to her by kerosene light,
Huck Finn's adventures, two years spent
before the mast, *Bleak House* and *Little
Women, Great Expectations*, and the Count of
Monte Cristo escaping from his cell
in Great-grandma's rough-milled, wind-creaking
moss-robed house, wreathed by second growth
woods, warblers and owls. And I

have been there ever since
on the slab-wood seat of the wagon,
gazing into the sun, dust and snow
and the trail behind where my people
sell sausages in Cologne, hide their
children in cellars, and huddle
against my grandfather's bombs,
and the trail ahead, where I walk
holding a grandchild's hand, looking
for hideouts of our history, tracks
not yet overgrown.

WHERE YOU COME IN

for F.P.

On my side of the world, I'm eleven and riding
my blue Raleigh to school. Seattle is a fine place
to raise children and you haven't even been born yet
in Sydney. So picture this boy pedalling fast
on an early empty street toward the all-American dream
of baseball on the school field before teachers arrive
and later in Yankee Stadium where DiMaggio
had won, then lost, Marilyn's heart.

Clenched in my bike rack, the leather mouth
of a glove that my hand has taught to whisper
small but growing miracles to the ball tucked inside.
And an ebony French clarinet from the German-
American grandmother whose son rode uncannily
unscathed through the war then was shredded by shrapnel
and shrouded in leather upholstery of his smashed
car, with his friends, nine months after

he saw me emerge from my mother. So safe,
the streets of Seattle, this isn't Bombay or Rome, so
from where did the car that hit me from behind,
which I didn't hear, a dark Houdini behind
the wheel, materialize? Imagine
this boy, still spinning but wobbling
out of control, hitting the curb, catapulted
upright like Da Vinci's Vitruvian Man

spread-eagled into a tree. Dr. Chesley later
would tell me, *You're lucky you didn't lose
your manhood* and I was lucky I didn't
understand. Why the car from nowhere
wouldn't stop, rolling casually down the road.
Study the boy splayed half in tulips
beneath the tree, half in the gutter, bike twisted,
clarinet case shocked open, emptied

of its broken bones, his glove where his limp
hand can touch it. Feel free to yell
fuck you when several cars slow,
drivers gawking – is that boy low-class
and drunk, crazy and rabid, epileptic and gross –
then drive on. Say *thank god* when a business-like
woman, maybe a break-through accountant or lawyer,
stops and says, *What on earth*

are you doing there? And I try, suddenly
much older, to say, *Are you blind and stunned, madam?*
I'm gasping for breath, mouth oozing blood, a comet's
tail of fire down my throat, ribs and groin.
Yet somehow knowing what matters most, she wedges
my bike in her trunk, gathers my glove and clarinet,
and as she lifts me into her car, I point to my baseball
down the street. *No*, she says, *you can easily get another.*

And this is where you come in. All the way
from Sydney, Aussie, ocean swimmer,
with no coordination of hand and eye,
avoiding objects batted, kicked or thrown.
Hearing this tale, you stroke across
the room and all these years I've wondered
why those drivers would not stop –
scoop up my baseball, drop it in my glove,

dolphin bearing the floundering
boy to shore.

PILGRIMAGE

for Tomás Gayton

When I was sixteen, I bought a sweater
for my girlfriend in Sak's Fifth Avenue,
cashmere, twilight blue. My first girlfriend
and first time in New York. I was in awe of
myself, shopping in that palace with heirs
to the throne Manhattan always seemed

to a kid from Seattle. She was blond,
swank, a whole year older, and owned
a T-bird convertible, a gift for graduation
from her father, a banker, descendant
of the Drambuie clan. The holy sacrament
was in my future, altar boy with aspirations

for the priesthood. I was travelling
all summer with Father Kappas, his first
long holiday in thirty years, and a pilgrimage,
and Anglican, meaning I could have sex
and marry and still say mass. I played
football too, with Tomás, best friend, fellow

aspirant and pilgrim, mentor
flinging books my way
and bodies from his all-star path
to college on an athlete's scholarship
then the seminary we visited in Wisconsin,
all those men in black absorbing

extra-terrestrial powers. In Green Bay,
next, we stayed with Father Kappas'
first bishop, who revealed a miracle:
his neighbour was Bart Starr, the Packers'
famous quarterback, who showed us
his study, his playbooks, his wisdom

and grace that shepherded teammates
to the promised land, and the field
next day where, inside heaven's earthly gate,
we watched a pantheon of gods
in pads and sweats run pass patterns and sprints.
Who needed Catholics and Notre Dame?

Then back in time, to a woods-secluded
monastery in Michigan, where we sang
Gregorian chants with Anglican monks, blazed
trails for meditation through their woods,
and, evenings, tasted Kierkegaard, Sartre,
and Jung in their startling spiritual cuisine.

Phone calls to Miss Drambuie Ancestor
once a week, her quests for water-skiing glory
on the lake, top-down rides of sun-tanned
joy to her island cottage and partying
with not-so-virgin-daiquiri sorority sisters
and frat rats from Greek row. And almost

every night, the piercing stigmata
of jealousy, primed to be wounded
self-esteem, vinegar and gall of fancied
betrayal. I was saved by Chicago,
and swallowed the lure there one night
of pagan temptation in a jazz club,

those hooks, those scales beginning to tip me
toward the promised, swinging land of soul.
But first, the honeyless, arid expanse
of Toronto, a world gathering of Anglicans,
bishops in dazzling robes, the Archbishop
of Canterbury, dull speeches, and I drifted off

to the tales Tomás told me of knights and gluttonous
monks, the Wife of Bath pricking my libido.
After those grand processions, we proceeded
to Montreal, men in berets, speaking *French*,
women like foreign movie stars, couples kissing
in public. Father Kappas meeting impishly

it seemed, with Roman Catholic friends.
This was where my father was born, and lived
for sixteen of his twenty-eight years,
and I looked for signs of what his death
had deprived me, of where I belonged.
Then Manhattan, and the revelation

of Sak's, Sir Boyfriend seeking the Holy Grail,
a wise young man bearing cashmere gifts.
Nothing else I recall of New York.
But that hot humid night in Ohio, Tom and I,
unable to sleep, threw our football
in the motel parking lot, cicadas and nighthawks

buzzing. With the name of the Rose, Jimmy
Rose, backup to a backup on the football team,
now my replacement, my now ex-
homecoming queen announced on the phone
near Little Big Horn. Tomás and I were reading
Nietzsche, Tomás the superman, not me. *Birth*

of Tragedy from my soul's sad music.
And Hugh Hefner's columns headed
his "Philosophy," and those ads:
"What kind of man reads *Playboy*?" White-
suited dude in a Jaguar with Chivas
Regal, a blond on each arm, a Churchill cigar.

We were careless, Father Kappas saw it, said
nothing. I felt empty as the landscape
of Montana which, years later, Miss Drambuie
angst transcended, would be a holy land, one
of many rich with parables, with nourishing
manna offered by countless minds.

Father Kappas, afraid of earthly heights,
lay down in the backseat through mountain
passes, voice rising with calming recitations
of *The Imitation of Christ*. Tomás and I intently
listening, that night, to the Ford Falcon's radio
as Sonny Liston knocked out Floyd Patterson.

I write this to Tomás, now a poet in La Jolla
and civil rights lawyer, just back from performing
in Habana. I'm in Cuba, too, ordained
by the waves, watching the dazzling procession
of bodies absolved by the sun, walking
to a scruffy field for the communion

of baseball with amigos. Father Kappas
retired to San Francisco, his mission
done, but without his two favourite acolytes
blessing the chalice. Yet we began, with him
as guide, to see the world as sacrament,
and every word a confession of faith.

Cayo Coco, 2006

ALAMO

I

The train stops at Mount Vernon.
History is new to me
and I am somehow confused and looking
for Thomas Jefferson's colonial home,
freed slaves, three thousand
miles northwest of Virginia. Following
my guardians through the dingy depot, then
peering out the mud-splattered
window of a smoke-filled bus to
Sedro Wooley. Doesn't that sound
like a place where crazy people go?
Heads full of lost sheep.
Faces and bodies drooping,
so unlike my crayon drawings in aqua blue
with white sailboats that never capsize,
airplanes and cars and mothers that
don't break down.

II

At school, when you do something
screwball that no one thinks funny
some kid might say, *You oughta get sent
to Sedro Wooley.* I cringe
when a classmate asks, *Where's your
mother?* Out sailing, she was
struck by lightning.
Mountain climbing she fell
off a cliff. She'd warned me about black
widow spiders, then got bit herself.
Maybe she's in Sedro Wooley, one
mean kid said. I coloured his face
nosebleed red, punched his mouth
so hard its alphabet wouldn't form
those ugly words again.

III

Welcome to Northern State Hospital.
Vast lawns groomed to
the equanimity of baseball fields.
Fireworking azaleas and rhododendrons.
Mallard-rippled ponds and orderly
line-ups of ornamental cedars and
a gazebo with merry-go-round horses
painted on its walls.

On a real diamond and outfield
ordinary-looking men play ball
as if they aren't insane. Beyond
the baseball: greenhouses and acres
of gardens, women bend, arms dangling,
hands busy below the knees.
I look for my mother but all of them are
wearing shapeless flower-print dresses,
straw hats or kerchiefs, their faces
shadows aimed at the ground.

They rebuilt the Alamo here, that period
craze for adobe walls, clay-tiled roofs,
a half-dozen huge fake mission-style buildings
with windows like the ones that Davy
Crockett shot through on TV. Arms
outstretched, St. Francis on the lawn,
but birdless, unlike the old whacko
man at Seward Park with his communion
of stale bread, his crusty chattering.

IV

We were starving, we went straight to the Hub,
the hospital's public café. The people
raising me ordered hot turkey sandwiches
and a cross-eyed waitress later brought
fruitcake with hard sauce. All patients,
said my mother's mother, meaning those
who served us, dishwashers and cooks, and
that made me wonder, would I be
poisoned? The wide pearly
doors to the kitchen flopped open,
the plump goose of my mother
walked through, her blubbery tears
at the sight of her boy,
rubber-gloved hands on my face
wet and squeezing.

V

Or she is not working and after dessert
a ward nurse guides us down a long
linoleum corridor like the aisle
of an almost bankrupt department store,
its lady clerks despondent
on sofas, wistful in rocking chairs,
standing fearful against the walls,
their visions of necklaces and perfumes,
their acrid outbursts
at customers who never come.

At the corridor's end, where the loco
motion in the cells of the Alamo
begins, we wait, my mother praying
we'll take her home this time, while outside,
the Mexican army advances, thousands of
thick moustaches, rifles and bayonets.
My mother checks her make-up
not suspecting how her son will die
bravely to save her.

WHAT MY MOTHER SAYS ON THE NURSING HOME PHONE

I drank two Diet Pepsis today,
is that bad? I'm not painting any more

pictures, the nurses can give my water
colours away. I've said that before,

haven't I? Many times? Maybe
my paintings will be famous someday and

we'll be rich. I auditioned for radio
when I was twelve. Mother dressed me up

pretty and took me downtown to the studio.
I loved that shiny microphone, but the man

said my voice wasn't cute enough. Jazz
was always my favourite music. Since my

stroke, I haven't played piano. I'm quitting
smoking after today. Father just loved

his Camels, said he'd gladly walk a mile
to buy a lovely lady like me a pack. When are you

coming to visit? Next spring? You should
see my new permanent, you'll be proud

that I paid for it with my monthly cheque. I got
banned from bingo because I cussed out

June, this Vietnam woman who keeps taking
that coffee mug you sent me. Father hated when

I swore, he was a hero, an Air Force major
and made me stand at attention for hours

when I was bad. My roommate Elora's
real nice, she never talks, just stares

at her TV. You going to spend Christmas
with your wife's family? Staying home?

The Japanese shot down your father's plane
in the war. They didn't? Oh. Those shoes

you sent me fit real well, but I could use
more white tennis socks. Do you still play

football? No? I forgot, you're getting old too.
Your mother's no spring chicken and my memory

keeps forgetting how to turn itself on but
anyway, you're still my sonny boy.

When's spring? May? How far away
is that? We can go to Value Village

then drive to the harbour and see
the boats sail away to the islands.

THE DAY AFTER

What I miss about church
are the candles, not the elegant
tall tapers on the altar, but the small
red lights at the feet of Mary.
Not the outstretched hands, her soft
face looking down, enfolding
blue-white robes, but the crimson
glass flickering like your eyes
with sunset the first time we walked
and touched on the seashore.

You were telling me your mother loved god
so much, you flattened yourself to live
inside the soundproof walls
between her prayers. You found,
escaping, the air outside was helium;
you let all the sandbags of scripture
go and haven't stopped soaring since.

I was aloft on frankincense,
an altar boy swinging the censer
to high heaven, sweet clouds
obscuring the sombre yet lurid
stations of the cross girding the pews.

Outside the church, I lost sight
of that god, his followers craving
forgiveness for the sins of being
human, thirsting for blood
transfusions. The sun hemorrhaging
light into the evening sea was sacrifice
enough, and its dawn resurrection
over the mountains a baptism
of fire. Rain lit the incense
of cedar and fir, and I woke to
the ruby-throated miracles
of hummingbirds, of a woman's wings,
like yours, beating so fast, hovering,
they were invisible. The angels

were never around when they needed
to be. Now, the day after my mother
left her body for good, vanishing
behind last night's full moon, you
fill the room with flames, tea lights
they're called, in small glass holders,
that I still know as votive candles,
each one a prayer, your hands
with their haloes upon me.

FOR YOUR LOSS

The difficulty of accepting
others' ways of grieving

the difficulty of explaining
one's grief to others

the griefs that meet in the street
between bullet-pocked buildings

and speak the same language
through crosshairs, on stretchers

the throats raw from wailing
and the lips that barely quiver

the dirge hammered on the anvil
of the ear, soft sighs in its labyrinth

the days dressed flawlessly in black
the shot glasses filled, and smashed

the grief that uproots a forest
or waters a garden where nothing

before now would grow, that offers
its breast to any parched mouth

that grinds the tongue to a gleaming
blade, that sinks so deep in a stone

no Merlin foresees its extraction
that issues forth from the flames

and smoke of the burning house
with photographs, wedding rings, flesh

slowly healing, a mesh of scars
a safety net for high-wire artists

who balance their grief for our upturned gaze
for our gasps, held breath, as they fall

NEWLY DEAD

Bombs go off in London
and I've not heard from you.
Twenty-two years since
I kissed you goodbye at
Heathrow security and ran for my life
back to Canada, the year Stan Rogers
died in a plane fire, rescuing others.
You knew his songs, slipped "Forty-Five Years"
into your Irish set-list on tour in Europe,
"Make and Break Harbour" for British pubs.

Fifty-six dead from the blasts. Elisabeth
Kübler-Ross dead for several years now.
She's how we met, at her workshop
on dying and death, the final stage
of this jig and reel and next leap
on the pilgrimage you believed
commences when souls emerge
incandescent in creation's fires.
What would she say of suicide
bombers? Their snapdragon
bouquets of shrapnel
faith, raucous birds of paradise
they bear in knapsacks
strapped to their disposable bodies?

Elisabeth and eighty black and red souls
in St. Alban's monastery outside London.
Black for the pitch and tar of unresolved
grief, red for vampire
anger. Before we were allowed
to vent, she told us to draw
a picture using boxes of crayons.
My cop-out green tree, blue sky
she glanced at, dismissed,
I thought, while your purple auroras, comets
streaking yellow as your hair, and orange
ibises gliding she held aloft for all of us

to see: spiritual longing, embrace,
transfigured heart unfolding.
I so, briefly, resented
you. And the Iranian woman fiercely
imperious in knee-high red boots and tight
black dress; her father
mutilated by the Shah's clean-shaved
thugs; a mullahs' bearded truth squad
bullet in her husband's head. *No white
space left on her drawing, see? no
room for healing, right?* asked Elisabeth. Not
yet. Or the virginal sheet with coils
and nooses, handcuffs in white crayon
we strained to see: the clench-faced
teacher's memory of taking his book-reading
eyes off his son, on the sidewalk, one moment
long enough for a speeding taxi to end it all.
I wanted to be that destroyed
by my losses, it suddenly seemed shallow
to have survived, intact, to have prospered.
Or, better, to be lambent
as you, glowing gold
rendered from Ireland's grim
ecstasies – morose, mellifluous, sluggard
alchemy. So I'd be chosen, transmuted,
raised up like a chalice
by Elisabeth's hands.

Nightfall, I defused the envy; by morning's
group session, I felt the scalpel voices
slice between my heart's
ribs, my companions one by one
sitting, no freezing, at the good doctor's feet.
Elisabeth's forceps clamped the flesh
open on what was arrested, on what was beating
them. To death. Her other instruments:
a pillow, tissues, fat London phone books.
I clung to my chair, modelling
empathy and rapt absorption, roles

I had no need to rehearse –
day one, two, morning three: watching
Vivian scrape out the plaque of her
husband's boozy death. Malcolm cauterize
the end of his guilt for the cigarette
left burning. Shirley rip into oblivion
a London phone book and the thickness
of her uncle's marauding hands.
Mehri from Iran scream bite and wail
into a pillow then pull off her boots
and dance, before us all, twirling
Elisabeth's lavender scarf. Elisabeth
sutured closed the teacher's chest
after he forgave himself
and life, its trespasses.

And you at Elisabeth's feet
for your father, voice like yours
the amber of Irish ale, but the songs
broken glass in his throat
since a Bloody Friday bombing on a Belfast road,
sister and brother-in-law dead.
Elisabeth's hand on your head and her face,
I swear, drawing strength from you.

I could no longer be
a compassionate observer. Moved forward,
sat cross-legged, intending to grieve
for my grandfather, murdered
in his tavern for a few bucks and change.
Surprise. I strangled
the pillow, slammed my fists into
the man who pulled the trigger
wherever the fuck he was hiding,
unidentified, never captured.
That morning, I did my best
to kill him. Then looked up, bewildered,
ashamed, at Elisabeth, who simply
nodded *yes* – whose face said, *Good,
that's out, now move on.*

Fourth night, a bonfire,
a basket of pine cones. Throwing one
to the flames, one heart-stone
cast away. Elisabeth asked me
to usher those in need of a guide
to the fire. What did *I* turn into
smoke and ashes? You
cradled your cone, a tiny child
you had to sacrifice. Your anguish
glimmering. I saw
the sorrow leave your face
like a heron rising
from a sundown shore.

Final morning, Elisabeth bringing
wine and chalice, asking me again
to serve. Communion. I would not do this
alone. This honour, undeserved. I asked
for you, and was granted
your hand cradling mine as we held
the chalice out for our companions.

Why choose me, not you?
I asked, green tea steeping, in the London flat
your widowed father bought
for you, sapphire-voiced Celtic troubadour.
My backpack on your floor. You radiate
love, I said, pollen on all our flowers,
sunlight after pitch-black rain.

But I'm frightened by others' bad dreams,
while you entered each person's nightmare
and wove your listening into ropes
they could grasp if they needed.

That rope was all Elisabeth, I said.

No, she doesn't work alone.

I was gathering material, I said, like Heaney
wrote, "artful voyeur," sympathetic, ruthless
user. *That too*, you said, grinning and binding
my hands to your breasts.

Next day's afternoon light and fresh
bread baking woke me, bathed citrine
in your bed. Wine, your flesh,
and warm loaves we tore with our hands.

In a Glasgow church basement
chain-smoking Elisabeth told eighty
new red and black souls:
Grief may last one year then
you must let the loved ones go or they become
carnivorous. Let them be
free to choose to visit you.
Anger is invaluable
for one minute at most then
clots in the brain's third eye,
soft words will cease,
darkness metastasize, and blind

impulses will, I add now, order hands
to strap explosives to the body.

You last saw me
running down an airport tunnel, late
from holding you too long.
If I turned, looked back, I would stay
and staying, leave everything
I knew, and I was not ready
for that, nor to fight the inertia
of my chosen path, nor the way
I gleamed in your arms, feathers of sunlight.
Now I choose to believe
that green tea is steeping in the afternoon
light, in your flat, and Elisabeth
there with the newly dead.

FAITH, HOPE AND

What if faith is a knife
stabbed through your hand, so cold-tempered,
so primordial, the blood
petrifies like amber, trapping
the insect of doubt inside.

What if faith disrupts your life
like your ancestors' *aboiteaux*
giving way, so that when the flood
waters recede, the sun bakes
pyramids of mud above uncertainty

and archaeologists wonder
at empty shrouds and grotesque
markings on amulets and shards.
What if hope is what you owe
the animals and plants you've plundered,

skinning the earth's rank pelt
so you could arc with desire
until your bones, your neurons glow
with isotopes your own walled city
cannot contain. You melt

down and the pilgrims to whom you lied
about your empty vault, camp
around your fires, asking not for pity
but for the byzantine trap
of your mouth to open wide.

What if the next word you speak
is not charity but anvil or torque
or shape-shifter, escape hatch, velocity.
What if the canyon echoes back
pass, through mountains, unvanquished peak.

BERLIN FOLLIES

DALÍ IN FLORIDA

(Salvador Dalí Museum, St. Petersburg, Florida)

I could swim in this light,
the blown-glass sky
and mother-of-pearl water
in St. Petersburg harbour. Too little breeze
for Christopher Columbus to come ashore
with his shipment of crosses
for aspiring churches and sprawling
malls; his descendants' armada of
yachts loll and quiver
in their impressionist moorings.

What are Salvador and I doing
here? Florida, the fountain of youth
haven for Canadians whose clocks have frozen
and need melting. True, roseate
spoonbills prowl the marshes, a long tail
of pristine seashore flicks behind the dragon
fire at Cape Canaveral, where
if I trick and treat myself
I can see Christ of St. John of
the Cross blasting off from
both Salvador's old world
crisis of faith and his well-healed
Florida patron and museum home.

I've been drawn here
by my wife's yearning
to blend her childhood and my stoned
adult memories of the Magic Kingdom:
how her father said he wants to come back
as a pelican skimming the surf;
how I became, at the Wild Ride wheel,
the inimitable Toad, oblivious to
commodification. The dominant theme
parks from which we've escaped, into the glare

of Dalí's barren landscapes pinging off a cranial harp,
an auto-sodomized virgin, the oh-so-clever artist
clipping his father's Freudian beard while
fragmenting a whole culture's memory.

I had never been attracted to his carnival
of atonement before, but now
my wife, seduced, stands behind
his wife, who leans out their villa
window overlooking the water, a sailboat
in the distance, Gala's back to her husband's
brushes and canvas; the landscape beyond
could be Florida, but the light
emanates from Gala's blouse and skirt,
the ripe aplomb of a woman who knows other women
will unenviously adore her in the presence of
their dumbstruck and delirious men.
This painting is different, old-fashioned,
tender, serene. The rest

is cannibalism, apotheosis,
extravagance for posterity, conquistadores
lunging ashore to convert
their caravels into car parks
centuries hence, Christ staring down
from the cross at golf shirts and Wonderbras.

Some epiphanies epoxy you: immobile,
you know there's another stained
glass window framed in the walls
through which you gawk at the world
and which rainbows your rooms with revelations.
The presence of Dalí in Florida:
startling, but just another conquest
of the irrational, no more surreal than
Pirates of the Caribbean, Gator Bowls,
and gun-in-the-glove-compartment euphoria.

Outside the museum, I know young Salvador
painted this harbour, in The Tower Mill studio
Ramón Pitchot provided. Before the break
with his father, the Church, the softer
impressions of forerunners who saw too much
in pastel waters, hazy bathers, shimmering
smoky afternoons, commerce distanced and
stilled. Before all the amputated
symbols, and before God the prosthetic.

Along a pier, facing the harbour,
I am brushstrokes on this canvas,
my back to my wife and her disposable
camera. Bemused to be so
placid in this milky affluent sublime,
gazing at tax shelters, and photographed
beside his monied benefactors' monument
to a fountain of eternal enigmas
of flamboyant desire.

IN THE VINCENT PRICE ROOM, JOURNEY'S END

Undertakers to Meet
  –The Guardian [Charlottetown, PEI] July 19, 2001

What do undertakers talk about
when they meet? Do they share the black
humour of anaesthetists, that exacting
routine punctuated by moments of sheer terror
when false teeth are lost or a spouse
glows with white-hot anger at a death-grimace
no art could remove or, at least, lacquer?
Do they practice those fastidious
makeovers on each other?
Rehearse those hushed voices, gently
touching their colleagues' elbows?

Or gather in sound-proofed convention
rooms and strike Chinese gongs, drink
Tequila sunrises and play
giddy rounds of paper, scissors, rock?
Perhaps they massage each other's delicate
hands, those manicured fingers blessed
by the angel of death, with the tact
and sure precision of surgeon and beautician.

I have come to believe they flirt and pair
off in their rooms and undress, a slow seductive
shedding of charcoal suits
and skirts, stiff white blouses and shirts,
underwear flimsy, sheer, vermillion,
never taking *la petite mort* lying down
but upright, defying gravity.

Though some never touch, only their eyes
ferrying back and forth across the river.

Walking past them down the hotel corridor
I hear one mention ashes on the Ganges.
Or is it managing their assets?

If I crashed their workshops, would I discover
them practising those soft, deep, compassionate
sounds, or training to suppress laughter?
In the session on "Understanding Grief"
do they meditate on photos of their late
fathers, ailing mothers, or tirelessly enact
the Monty Python dead parrot skit?

They must shop-talk about us,
the mourners. Rate our bereavement,
swap designations: weepers, eye-dabbers,
zipper-lipped, morbid.
And surely they must complain
about music, how they hate
hearing "Nearer My God to Thee."
How they long to crank up "Sympathy
for the Devil" or "You ain't
nothing but a hound dog," or instruct
the organist to play "Stairway to Heaven"
backwards. Late in the evening,

in the hospitality suite, they drink
shooters they call embalmers,
and with a flushed, self-conscious thrill
play "Name the Immortals."
Then push each other over the brink
of remembrance: the devastated,
the forlorn they could not console.
That done, they make lists.
Hymns that permeate even the brass
and varnished wood of their hearts.
Handshakes that made them tremble.
Moments alone with the dead
when the room's air thins and parts,
the mind wavering, light-headed,
as if someone has drawn a boost
from the brain's electricity, recharged
and sped off, the lights briefly dimmed,
air quivering, then still.

MEDITATION IN THE GARDEN IN THE GULF

I

Do I believe in anything enough
to kill? I am not thinking of self-
defence on this spring morning, sun
steaming open the envelop of earth,
birch trees ruffling their fledgling feathers
outside my window awash with a harbour,
where wooden warships or iron, turreted
leviathans appear only on web sites,
postcards in antique shops on this island
peaceful for two hundred years.

Where homicides in any decade
can be counted on one or two hands –
a priest killed by two young men
surprised while robbing the offering;
a woman strangled on a hiking trail;
cold case of a gay teacher, smeared
in (jealous or vengeful?) blood; wives
who found shelter from husbands
in a coffin.

II

I'm thinking of that blinding
light of conviction that blows
martyrs up to their heaven; that airlifts
cocoons of fire to camps and towns,
those billowing moth-dark clouds
of souls; that steadies the sniper's gun;
that lines the unbelievers up
like soccer players facing a penalty shot.
Or the common leap or belly crawl
or charge among ten thousand men
yoked in their greater DNA of good.
I could say *Hitler* and *Nazis*
as we often do. And who wouldn't

blast the Borg, barely human, really?
Facile. But, here and now, when birdsong
vanishes from prairies, farmers
wonder at the empty hives, the permafrost
is honeycombed with tracks, and tankers
dock in this tranquil harbour
to fill our four-wheel mouths, I raise
only the finger flag, faith lacking
in the lasting beauty of a creed's
lethal weapons. Or too content among
these candling chestnuts, their confetti
in the breeze. On this island, blessed
by irrelevance, by the spoils of bloodshed
elsewhere.

Prince Edward Island

BRIDE OF THE CAPTURED EARTH

After a painting by Charles Malinsky

Imperious, naked, triumphant, she sits
astride an enormous, enfeebled, white
rhino, its huge horned head
thrust forward, but drooping
beneath her axe-blade face
raised and gleaming, the diamond
drills of her breasts. Her thighs
grip that hide, creased, sere,
tough yet now penetrable
as the hymens of the wrong prophet's
women when Jerusalem was taken.

Borne aloft, that beast, and groaning,
staggering beneath its weight are epic
men, their rippling, fierce, erotic
agony almost enviable, that moment
miles forward when they falter,
buckle, are crushed. The necessary
scornful centurions, trimmed beards
and spears, flank, prod, ennoble
this procession, their eyes
piercing the distance
between now and nothing. She is
impervious to the muscles straining,
the moans of remorse, below, and only
her lips, protuberant,
succulent as eels, betray
her insatiable, nuptial kiss.

FREELY, SING

Forget gendered neurochemistry and alpha
male theory and psychopathology.

They come from another planet,
galaxy, dimension. Shape-shifters

or body snatchers, they assume the fleshy
semblance of leveraged buyout brokers,

the LED light aura of those who speak
for unfettered markets, affordable labour

costs and shiny bubbly stuff.
They're immunized against

the viruses of certain artists' rants,
conclusions of scientists on the wrong

payroll, and those motivated by
injury, perceived injustice, unfortunate loss.

Entering our emotional atmosphere
with heat-shield certitude, they disarm us

with their calculus of hope. Cyber-
psychics, they channel our feverish

or soporific imaginings into infinite-
ringed circuses ever-arriving in town.

Or, when the glass dome shatters and floors
cave in, their grave, soothing voices

transmitted from distant stars say,
think how worse it would be without us:

contemplate the gradual relief we bring
from the long history of inevitable pain

or, if you prefer, release, from crops,
cubicles, assembly lines and loading docks

to bliss, eternal.
Their weaknesses: our still primitive

techniques, which constrain them;
their unwavering faith in their logic;

unsettling vibrations when we, too
freely, sing.

AFTER THE STARSHIPS

After the starships departed
we gazed at the sky for hours, then glanced
upward for days. *Just like a dream,*
one famous actor said on a talk show,
British accent more sublime, midsummer
night's face glowing, ethereal,
where the most ravishing person
begins to make delicate love to me
then vanishes. A ravenous, alien
emptiness lodged inside us,
and we were sucked into the gravity
of those who had felt something
like this before: parents
with children beamed out by cancer,
by riptides, by speeding cars; children
whose parents were voodooed away
by dementia; people dazed and picking
through the rubble, after the tremors,
the water and wind, explosions and flames,
for fragments of home amidst the mud
and shrapnel. Or those levelled and lacerated
so differently, by the backwash of bliss,
filled to bursting with the dullness after
one fleeting night with a perfect lover,
the trek to the ultimate peak or waterfall,
the deed for which they were lifted
on jubilant shoulders,
the sapphire voice, for an instant,
that might have been god.

They were not deities, or emissaries
of immortals, though several were gifted
with radiance in their translucent brains
which let them journey to a cosmos
where spirits resembling honeybees
danced and distilled our universe
from their hives of golden fire.
Die-hard skeptics stopped sneering.
When we touched the hulls, our hands

slipped inside a warm enchantment
and we were gripped in a moment of birth,
were potters molding wet clay,
farmers up to our wrists in spring soil.
Even those of us who believed in nothing
before or beyond
stopped frowning,
looked in the travellers' eyes,
could see ourselves in all
the refractions of light and were beautiful.

LOAD AND LOCK

Fire and wire, the neurophysicist said. *For example*,
when she says not to talk so soon
after sex, and you clench your jaws and come
to a boil inside for the umpteenth time, your synapses
are building a white-hot bridge of crackling
impulses you'll be suspended on.
But when she descends on the parachute of Friday
night, removes the shoes
that mean business when they speak with tight
restraint across the thirty-third floor, and asks you
to rub her feet, if your hands make her body
a lazy river your fingers float down
beneath the lunar eclipse of her eyes, then her cell
receptors will load and lock the neuropeptides of
contentment where her body spills.

At the sub-atomic level, particles are infinite
possibilities, waiting for you to act and
react to her pick of movies, friends for
Thanksgiving dinner, carnal positions. Arm
those synapses often enough with champagne
corks or shrapnel and she'll open herself
for bubbly or brace herself for bits of steel.
The choice, after rehearsing alternate lines
in the quantum wings, listening to the voices
and white noise of neurotransmitters stationed
throughout the audience, and judging the distance to
the gun mounted above the fireplace mantle, is yours.

ACTAEON

Be still now: listen.
     – "Siren," Fiona Ann Papps

I was not hunting that day. I only drew blood
when other young men, teeth crowding their
smiles, shamed me away from the clay my hands kept

shaping into flawless imperfections of the women
those quivering trees in my dreams were embracing.
I was fleeing my father, my friends' fathers, the season's old

wine loosening talk of stalking one beautiful woman after
another as they strolled through the courtyard, dropping them
to their knees with thick supple arrows,

watching their eyes roll back under lids, and before
their beauty could recoil, trap and destroy them, leaving seed
so deep it would sprout rhododendrons dripping mad honey.

Walking for hours, I lost myself in ripe green light
of cypresses, and thought they whispered *Go back
to the safety of oaks, goodness of olives, airy seductions of myrtles.*

But I had found my dream, my glade, a pond rippling
through my veins as I approached. And saw her, bathing, her moon
face pregnant with sun, a bear pendant

around her neck, and breasts that split my vision
open like a pomegranate. She glanced
at a quiver of silver arrows nearby

and stars circling her head grew brighter, so she moved
toward me, skin shedding moonstones and pearls.
Drew an arrow, strung it, aimed at my heart, and pulled.

Then laughed. Lowered her bow. It is true: the antlers and hoofs.
In my sudden brown hide, I stood unafraid, as she rubbed aloe
where the arrow grazed my flank. She draped her hair

over my antlers, her hand,
a crescent moon, sliding into my breast.
White light seared my heart. She took

my hand between her legs, and there was blood.
Not a virgin's, she said. *Do you want
me, now? Yes or no, either way I will spare you.*

I tell you this from a rocky island cave where the priests
won't find me. Where my father won't choke me with incense
and poison me with more lies. Where my friends won't insist

that the scar on my chest was from wrestling a wild boar
or a jealous Thracian whore. Or self-inflicted in my madness.
That the stains on my thighs are birthmarks, and always there.

CURTAIN

The day Pavarotti died
you sang "Nessun Dorma"
over the rap music blaring
from the neighbours' balcony.

You stood in the liquor store line
with Pinot Grigio, surrounded by *soi-disant*
Canadians bearing cartons of Coors and Bud
and sailing off with Captain Morgan.

You wore the red dress with cleavage
Luciano would have rapturously
serenaded, and gold-trimmed high heels
to board the barge on the Nile of your patio.

You made pesto for the entire chorus,
and pasta that delayed Radames
from his grand entrance. Buzzing
with your espresso, the orchestra

raced through Aida's death scene,
while the great tenor dabbed at his brow
with his white handkerchief, leaned back
in your lawn chair, savouring the wine.

When he departed, bowing, and kissing
your hand the final time, you drifted
down the Nile until the full moon set,
past the pyramids, past Alexandria,

out on the sea past the Sirens and toward
that peninsula where one voice rose
and burst and pulsated and was gone
behind the curtain of stars.

THE PURRING YOU HEAR

for J.L.

I

What if love is the music
your neurons fire when you fear
nothing, not even the startling, abrupt
frost on desire, the deep
freeze of rejection? Cooling your heels
alone at the altar your bed
once was, the scent of her too sacred
to launder. Your underground economy
of sex diverted offshore,
pirates welcome
to seize your ship, set you adrift
on the raft of your heart's electric
currents. Not *m'aidez*,
not even thirsting, content to await
the next mirage
that sucks you into her whirlpool
arms, and you, a bundle
of thawed, parched neurons
swearing not to be another mutinous
sailor, vowing love's synaptic
lightning and twelve-toned
carnal notations of scars.

II

What if love is the evening star
leaking its light through your bedroom window
and shattering? Can you view
her more sharply, with more clarity
and compassion, her distortions not unlike
your own pierced perceptions of waves
and particles travelling through space
from all those suns you thought would burn
much longer, that wispy *forever*.
What if love is a shrike
impaling sparrows on thorns, or
an alabaster Egyptian urn
where the phoenix's ashes are interred?

III

What if love is a horse you ride
flat-out until it foams, stumbles, leg
broken, and you must turn your head
and pull the trigger?
Or a car you drive long after it's rusted,
engine still turning over on the coldest
dawns. Or the space station she's made of
her life, where she asks you to stay
for the night, or weeks, or revolutions
of moons. You gazed down
longing for gravity, then rocketed
back to the atmosphere and the bliss
of living alone, until one night you glide
sleepless in bed toward her orbiting
light and lust to be weightless.

IV

Around her gaze, the moon
is a field of white chrysanthemums.
The breeze plucks and sends them drifting
in the dark blue air to you. Breathing,
asleep, you dream petals glowing
phosphorescent. Your own sheen
and scent waking every pollen-seeker
for a thousand miles. A voice, wild,
dispassionate as the sea
nearby, says, Dreams are the day's
jetsam, moonlight sinks into the shore's
black rock and sucks the tides the way
the blood will rush to your head
if you think the clouds
are anything other than vapour.
The moon, amused, disagreeing, seeps
her tongue deep inside you, laps
the cream from the bowl of your heart.
What if the purring you hear
is love, its claws,
for now, furled?

BERLIN FOLLIES

I

Alone in Berlin, the only German word
I know my father's last name. Startled
by my mother's on this boulevard's signs,
Alexanderplatz. I'm waiting, looking
for one: a signal, password, beckoning
me through a doorway to a roomful
of not-strangers. A voice saying
I helped your ancestor, a butcher
in Jackaranth near Koln, flee the bloody
wars over god, the knives used to carve
up kingdoms and families in the way

of inexorable lusts. My companion
has a business meeting in Frankfurt,
another lover there too, the one who paints
himself and his women in stained glass
post-coital martyrdom, in airplanes with wings
torn off, dangling from tangled
parachutes. We have a mutual understanding
about sex. Not exactly light
housekeeping, as Billie Holiday said, more like
different mouthpieces for the same sax.
With her off in Frankfurt, my mind
at loose ends, words guttural, my own lust
in the way, I travelled deeper into the black
fabled forests of steel, faith, wolves,
cantatas, cabarets, the fire-bombed
leider leaking through beer-stein
bravado my Teutonic grandfather, posing
with his six-guns drawn, displayed
in his Minnesota cavalry uniform,
the Sioux threat crushed, the Spaniards next.

My companion, English, traces
her war with oppression back to Boudicca,
flogged, daughters raped, husband slaughtered,
enraged and spearing Roman colonists. How far
back should I go? My own British
grandfather dropping bombs on the Kaiser's
trench-doomed lads? The wild-maned men
heaping their deaths at the legions' feet?
Or just this black-and-chain-clad blond
Fraulein handing me a flyer for a protest
against my fellow American Frankensteins
cloning then disowning their creatures?
Je suis Canadien, I say to her, *maintenant*.
And my last name is (Dutch, last week
in Amsterdam) a four-letter word
like *Heil*, like lust, like Bach.

II

Next to a shop selling the freedom of
bondage, an African clothing boutique
and I'm smitten by the Sudanese owner,
goddess of long-necked, leaping
creatures, these fabrics, her own designs
I'd never wear, lacking courage
to dress in a way drawing stares
back home. But here, she says,
you can be who you are. Yeah
right. I am a closet
dancer who asks if there's a black
music club, hoping she'll say yes and
take me. But she and her partner
Ingrid have other plans. I go
alone.

A lonely white male at the bar
with my lager. I have stumbled into
the disco where black American GIs nurse
their fantasies of impossibly tall,
serpentine, lean, aloof
German women, their minimalist
movements hypnotic, electro-magnetic
fields we can't escape
or enter. I try, white boy
who learned to dance in my mixed race
neighbourhood, slick, supple, combustible,
short and egregious among these gothic
icy wonders. Slump and slouch
back at the bar with the others, adopt their look
of cool disdain and desire. Women like this
don't want men like me. I should be
lost in my journal in a bookstore café
where, no expectations, I'll be surprised
by a woman like Gina Cohen, left-wing
dentist's daughter, whose grandparents packed up
their troubles in an old kit bag the first time
they heard the Fuhrer's radio voice.
Gina turned on by my talk
to her social work students on refugee
kids I helped traverse through
the anomie of a strange land. I am
handed a beer by an Ethiopian
engineer named Klaus, né Kenenisa .
He is not here for the women. He misses
everything African, except the lack of
work, money, safety, good beer. Do I like
Marvin Gaye, Liza Minnelli or Cher?

III

In the city that never sleeps, I am walking
alone, longing for Gina, whom I dumped
for another child of Jewish émigrés,
her father born in Siberia, a Tsarist labour camp,
mother in a Polish shtetl, daughter melting
into Manhattan, then into me, hybrid, border
straddler, toddler in the archives
of who I am, telling cute poignant stories
of my past, sensitive, sub-cutaneous, might be
seductive gibberish to that New York woman's
state of mind, wanting out, wanting
pastoral, a gentle land, like Canada, a gentle

man, who, more women later, follows his father's
footsteps into the fatherland, armed
with a notebook, an American smile
for the drop-dead gorgeous spike-heeled
woman who stops, curious, sits at my three a.m.
café table, asks what I'm writing and quotes me
her prices. How much for shoving her tongue
down my throat, past my larynx, my heart,
to that place I've never learned
how to sing from
in any language? How much for love?
I love how she laughs, equal parts
neon, smoked meat, and soft black leather.
You look, she says, like you've had
more than your share, so good luck
getting fucked, and finding your ancestors.

IV

Back in Frankfurt, walking the platform
beside the train from Berlin, a uniformed man
leans out a coach's window, waving
a notebook. Is this yours?
You left it behind.

ACKNOWLEDGEMENTS

"Retribution" and "Patriots II: Softening" were published in *Malahat Review*; "Hendrix of Arabia," "I'll Be Gone" and "Five Things Disgusted Him" were published in *Grain*; "Load and Lock" and "Actaeon" appeared in *The Fiddlehead*; "Richard Speaks to Me, the Faint-Hearted" was published in *Arc*; "In the Vincent Price Room, Journey's End," appeared in *forgetmagazine.com*., and in *Going Down Swinging No. 29* (Australia).

Sincere gratitude to The Canada Council for the Arts for the generous support of an artist's grant to work on this manuscript. My appreciation, also, to the University of Prince Edward Island for sabbatical leave, which afforded additional time to write, and to the Tasmanian Writers Centre for a residency in Hobart.

I am deeply indebted to Barry Dempster, editor extraordinaire, for his astute, precise and wise editorial work on this manuscript. My deepest gratitude to the wonderful people at Wolsak and Wynn, Noelle Allen and Lindsay Hodder.

A special thanks to Lee Ellen Pottie, Melissa Carroll and Fiona Papps, who generously provided invaluable editorial advice and encouragement.

Richard Lemm is an award-winning author, and a professor of literature and creative writing at the University of Prince Edward Island. He has published four previous collections of poetry, a book of short fiction, *Shape of Things to Come*, and a biography of Canada's "People's Poet," *Milton Acorn: In Love and Anger*. His most recent poetry book is *Four ways of dealing with bullies* (Wolsak and Wynn, 2000). Born in Seattle, he immigrated to Canada in 1967, and moved to Atlantic Canada in 1979.

Aug